```
J                    4371878
914.7                   13.90
Fli
Flint
The Russian Federation
```

DATE DUE			

THE RUSSIAN FEDERATION

By
David C. Flint

The Millbrook Press
Brookfield, Connecticut

Reprinted 1993

© Aladdin Books Ltd 1992

Designed and produced by
Aladdin Books Ltd
28 Percy Street
London W1P 9FF

First published in the
United States in 1992 by
The Millbrook Press
2 Old New Milford Road
Brookfield, Connecticut 06804

The consultant is Dr. John Channon of the School of
Slavonic and Eastern European Studies, London, UK.

Series Design: David West
Designer: Rob Hillier
Editor: Suzanne Melia
Picture Research: Emma Krikler

Library of Congress Cataloging-in-Publication Data

Flint, David C.
    The Russian Federation/by David Flint :
    John Channon, consultant.
        p. cm – (Former Soviet states)
    Includes bibliographical references and index.
    Summary: Examines the economy, outmoded industries,
and other problems of the former Soviet republic of the
Russian Federation.
    ISBN 1-56294-305-7 (lib bdg.) :
    1. Russian S.F.S.R. –Juvenile literature. (1. Russian
S.F.S.R.)
I. Title. II. Series.
DK510.23.F55 1992
947'.–dc20   92-5737 CIP AC

Printed in Belgium

CONTENTS

INTRODUCTION

The Russian Federation is the largest and most influential state to emerge from the break-up of the Soviet Union. The old Soviet Union was created in 1922, following the October Revolution of 1917, which had established a communist government. However, in July 1990, Russia declared its independence within the Soviet Union, and on 12 June, 1991, Boris Yeltsin was elected president of the newly independent state.

Covering over 17 million square kilometres (6.5 million square miles), Russia extends south from the Arctic Ocean to the Black Sea, and east from the Baltic Sea to the Pacific Ocean. Following the break-up of the Soviet Union, eleven of the fifteen former republics agreed to form a loose alliance called the Commonwealth of Independent States, or C.I.S. The aim is to encourage trade between the member states, but power now rests firmly with each independent state, not with the C.I.S.

Arctic Ocean

Zemlya Frantsa Josifa

170° E
160° E
150° E
140° E
130° E
120° E
90° E
80° E
70° E

Severnaya
Zemlya

Novo Sibirskiye
Ostrova

Laptev Sea

Kara Sea

Kolyma

Bering Sea

Lena

Yenisey

RUSSIAN FEDERATION

Sea of Okhotsk

50° N

Sakhalin

JAPAN

Trans-Siberian Railroad

Lake Baikal

40° N

Vladivostok

MONGOLIA

NORTH KOREA

SOUTH KOREA

CHINA

| 0 | 250 | 500 | 750 | 1000 | 1250 MILES |
| 0 | 500 | 1000 | 1500 | 2000 KILOMETERS |

THE STATES TODAY

Eleven former republics of the defunct Soviet Union create the C.I.S., Dec. 21, 1991.

Because it is so big, covering such a huge land area, Russia is rich in natural resources, from oil and gas to lumber, gold and fish. In 1991 Russia produced 78.6 percent of all the Soviet Union's natural gas, 60 percent of its steel, 80 percent of its lumber and 91 percent of its oil. Russia can supply all its own needs as regards food and energy. It also has over 75 percent of all the former Soviet Union's industry. This wealth gives Russia a powerful position in relation to the other states of the C.I.S. If it chose to, it could call the economic shots completely. The C.I.S. has retained the ruble as a single common currency, but it does not have a central budget or common citizenship. Millions of Russians now live in "foreign" countries, such as the Ukraine and Kazakhstan, which were once extensions of their homeland.

The Russian flag flies over the Kremlin in Moscow

Wielding the upper hand?

The other states of the C.I.S. have to buy their oil and gas from Russia. It is the nearest large source of these vital power resources. In the past, the states paid very low prices for Russian oil and gas. This was one benefit of belonging to the Soviet Union, and it helped to bind the states together. Independence has begun to change this pattern. Now Russia can greatly increase the price it charges for its oil and gas. This would be very profitable and give it a large trade surplus. So far, however, Russian leaders have kept oil and gas prices low as an encouragement to other states to become members of the C.I.S.

Interdependence

If it chose to do so, Russia could manage its economy without buying much from the other states. However, Russia wants to encourage interstate trade, so it buys grain from the Ukraine and Kazakhstan, cotton and tea from the central Asian states, and ships from the Baltic states. In return the Russian Federation exports oil and gas to most of the other C.I.S. members, and to Latvia, Lithuania, and Estonia. These Baltic countries are wholly reliant on Russian energy sources. Russia is still the main source to other states of manufactured goods. These goods include such things as agricultural machinery, cars, railroad locomotives, computers, and steel.

Power struggles

Current disputes between C.I.S. members center on the price of goods exchanged in trade, and who controls the former Soviet army, navy, air force, and nuclear weapons. For example, Russia and the Ukraine disagree about who should control the powerful Black Sea naval fleet. Only if the C.I.S. can resolve such problems will it be able to function successfully in the future.

Moscow

Moscow is the capital of the Russian Federation, and is one of the largest cities in the world. More than eight and a half million people live in Moscow, which is a leading manufacturing center. Emerging as the most powerful Russian city in the 1400s, Moscow became the home of the Tsars until 1712 when the capital was moved to St. Petersburg. Moscow resumed its role as capital in 1918 after the Bolsheviks had seized Russia and set up a communist government.

Moscow has many beautiful buildings, including St. Basil's Cathedral, famous for its colorful, onion-shaped domes. The Kremlin stands at the heart of the city, an old fortress that became the focus of Soviet government.

Moscow has long been the center of Russian and international culture. The world renowned Bolshoi Theater presents operas and ballets that are ranked among the best in the world. Moscow also has many museums and art galleries. Moscow is also the center of Russian media and communications.

Problems that face the city include pollution, an increase in crime due to economic hardship, and a rise in the number of homeless.

PEOPLE AND PLACES

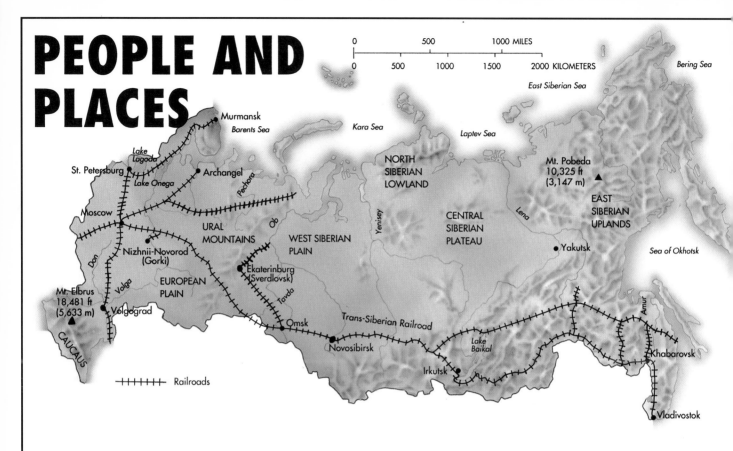

Railroads

Over 80 percent of Russians live in the western third of their country, centered around Moscow. The eastern parts of the country – namely Siberia and the Far East (eastern Siberia) – are vast empty tracts with hardly any people.

Because Russia is such a large country, there are many different ethnic groups, each with a language of its own. Russian, however, is the official language of the country.

A country divided

In Siberia and the Far East, people live close to the Trans-Siberian railroad, which is the main land link between eastern and western Russia. Recently the Baikal-Amur-Mainline (B.A.M.) railroad has been built parallel to the Trans-Siberian, but farther north. The aim is to open up these empty areas so that the iron ore, uranium, gold, diamonds, coal, lumber, and other resources can be sought out and developed.

Laying the last rails on the Trans-Siberian

Polluting Lake Baikal

Baikal, otherwise known as the "blue eye of Siberia," is the largest lake in Russia, and the deepest and oldest lake in the world. It holds one fifth of the world's fresh water. Its purity is due to the presence of a unique crustacean that devours bacteria. This purity, however, is under threat due mainly to the pollution created by a cellulose plant and many other factories that have poured waste products into Siberia's lakes and rivers.

The cellulose plant was built on the southern shores of the lake in 1961 in order to take advantage of the supply of pure water. The mill now pollutes its own source of water, and the affected area has spread to a zone of about 30 miles (48 kilometers), badly affecting the forests on the edge of the lake.

It is only since the arrival of *glasnost* (openness) in Russia that concern has been voiced over Baikal and many of the country's rivers. The Selenge River, which provides half of Lake Baikal's water, is also heavily polluted by factories. This river is the main breeding ground for the Siberian white salmon, unique to this area.

Campaigners for the environment in Russia have always been frustrated by the complete lack of antipollution laws in the former Soviet Union, and it is only recently that Lake Baikal has received the worldwide recognition that is more usually associated with issues such as the rain forests.

A legend states that a dip in Lake Baikal will make you look 12 months younger. Time for the lake, however, is running out.

The western part of Russia, by contrast, has all the country's large cities, 90 percent of its useful agricultural land, over 85 percent of its industry, and all its important decision-making centers. Russia is thus a country of two very

Lake Baikal, the "blue eye of Siberia"

unequal parts. Because the western area has been inhabited and developed for hundreds of years, many of its resources such as lumber, iron ore, and coal are virtually exhausted.

Untapped resources

These unused resources lie to the east in Siberia and the Far East, where environmental surveys indicate the presence of natural gas and oil. But while eastern Russia is rich in resources, it lacks the people. In the past, people were either forced to go and work in Siberia and the east, or were paid very high salaries to go there. The present government realizes that in the short term it must continue to pay people two or even three times the average salary to encourage them to work in Siberia. However, in the long term there are plans to improve rail and road links between the eastern and western regions.

FROM RUS TO RUSSIA

The history of Russia is to a large extent the story of an ethnic people called the Slavs who gradually brought other groups under their control. Between the first and ninth centuries A.D., the Slavic tribes developed agricultural and trading centers along rivers like the Volga and the Dnepr. They were regularly attacked by tribes such as the Goths and Huns from the south or the Vikings from the north. By 862 a leader called Rurik had established a small kingdom called Rus, with Novgorod as its capital. This kingdom was based in the northern forests and gradually expanded so that in 882 Oleg, Rurik's successor, had managed to capture the kingdom based at Kiev to the south.

Towns grew to be important economic and social centers. They were the bases from which parties controlled the area, kept out raiders, and stored the wealth they collected. Trade flourished in these towns, together with craft industries, and soon churches and cathedrals were built.

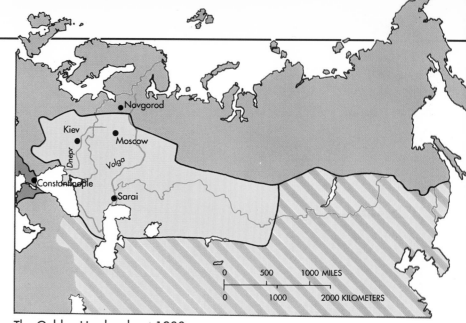

The Golden Horde—about 1300

	Golden Horde
	Other parts of the Mongol Empire
	Byzantine Empire
———	Present Russian border

The Golden Horde

During the thirteenth century, Mongol invaders from the south began attacking Rus. These horsemen had good military skills and in 1223 defeated the Slav forces, capturing Kiev in 1240. Rus became part of the Mongol Empire in a section called the Golden Horde. However, Novgorod remained independent and had trade links with Baltic countries specializing in furs. Novgorod was also the site of other battles against invaders.

The first Tsar

Around 1143, Moscow began to replace Novgorod as the nucleus of the new Russian state. It was at the meeting point of several trade routes based on land and river, and in 1326 the seat of the Metropolitan Orthodox Church was moved from Kiev to Moscow. Moscow continued to fight the Mongols (also called Tatars) under Ivan III, and after 1547 his successor, Ivan the Terrible, made Moscow his capital. He was crowned "Tsar," a title derived from the word "Caesar," and became grand prince of all Russia. He used a policy of

Tsar Ivan IV (the Terrible)

warfare and terror to conquer tribes along the Volga and so expand Russia southward. Ivan also formed a special police force, and began a reign of terror, ordering the arrest and the murder of hundreds of aristocrats. He also burned down towns and villages. It was during this time that Richard Chancellor, an Englishman, visited Russia. He founded the Muscovy Company to establish trade between England and Russia. He was successful in persuading Ivan to open the new port of Archangel in the north, to allow the export of Russian furs, gold, and diamonds.

The Cossacks
By the middle of the sixteenth century, the forest state of Russia had emerged as undisputed leader of the Slavs. To the south was a frontier area where the forest gave way to the grassy plains of the steppes. Here, semimilitary communities grew up, formed by people seeking freedom from serfdom in nearby Poland and Lithuania. They were the Cossacks, whose name means "free warriors," and were employed by the Tsars as soldiers to control conquered lands. Both Poland and Russia granted the Cossacks many privileges as a reward for their services. The Cossacks formed self-governing communities that were based on democratic principles. Most of the Cossacks then lived in an area that is now part of the Ukraine.

Siberian Cossacks patrol the newly conquered lands to the east.

During the short summers, the early settlers sailed eastward from Archangel to the Ob River.

THE CONQUEST OF SIBERIA

The Ural Mountains and the Ural River, which flows into the Caspian Sea, are usually taken to mark the boundary between Europe and Asia. In the first part of the sixteenth century, this was an important border between the Slavic civilization to the west and the Tatar civilization to the east. It was only after 1552, when the Tatar state of Kazan was captured, that the Russians could move eastward across the vast area known as Siberia. This was an area of forest, giving way to barren tundra in the north.

Taming a wilderness
Siberia has always been notorious for its long, bitterly cold winters. Temperatures in January commonly fall to -49 degrees Fahrenheit (-45 degrees Centigrade), and the ground remains permanently frozen all year. During the brief summers the top few inches of the soil thaw, and swarms of mosquitoes add to the discomfort of this huge, remote region. The early Russian settlers came in search of furs from animals like mink and sable which lived in the forests. The Stroganov family acquired new lands in Siberia from the Tsar, and sent a Cossack army to conquer and subdue the area. Their leader, Yermak, was killed in the fighting, and in 1585 a fort was built at Tyumen. A string of fortified trading

posts was built along the valleys of the Ob, Tobol, and Irtysh rivers.

A creeping empire

The early settlers suffered great hardships as they struggled to cross the 5,000 miles (8,046 km) of coniferous forest stretching across Siberia. Traders, trappers, soldiers, and administrators struggled along river valleys and forest trails from Moscow. Sometimes, in the short summers, they would sail from Archangel, along the Arctic coast to the mouth of the Ob River However, dangers such as shipwreck and attack from hostile tribes, made this route hazardous as well. The Cossacks usually pioneered the overland routes, while the traders and trappers dragged their heavy boats overland between eastward-flowing rivers. It was often easier to travel over the frozen snow and ice of winter than the mud of spring and autumn. They pushed on eastward, and in 1632 founded Yakutsk on the River Lena. Finally, in 1648, they fought their way across the mountain ranges of the Far East to reach the Pacific coast.

Siberia is notorious for its long, bitterly cold winters.

Unrealized wealth

Later, in 1699, the long peninsula of Kamchatka was colonized; this is an area studded with active volcanoes and prone to earthquakes. By the end of the 17th century, the Tsars had gained a huge empire wrapped around one third of the globe. Initially they were only interested in the wealth Siberia could provide in the form of furs, gold, and diamonds. Siberia's real strategic value was only recognized later.

The Siberian Taiga

This is the largest forest in the world. The Taiga extends across the entire Eurasian continent from Scandinavia to the Sea of Okhotsk. The forest is a mixture of larch, fir, spruce, and other conifers which support an abundance of wildlife. Animals of the Taiga include the brown bear, elk, musk deer, red squirrel, sable, fox, lynx, and weasel. Extensive as it is, the beauty of the Taiga is threatened by flash fires and deforestation.

THE ROMANOVS

Michael Romanov succeeded Ivan the Terrible in 1613 after Ivan had killed his son in a fit of rage. The new Romanov dynasty was to remain in control of Russia for the next 304 years. In 1689 Peter the Great, another Romanov, came to power. He was aware of the great scientific and technical progress being made in the countries to the west of Russia. He also recruited foreign

A portrait of Peter I (the Great), engraved by P. Pikart in 1707

engineers, surgeons, industrialists, and other specialists, persuading them to work in Russia and pass on their knowledge to others.

Building windows and opening doors

Peter had a new city built on swampland near the Baltic. He called it his "window to the west," and named it St. Petersburg. In 1712 Peter made St. Petersburg the capital, so the city grew as a port and as an industrial center. Peter introduced a system of elementary education, an Academy of Sciences, and a system of secret police.

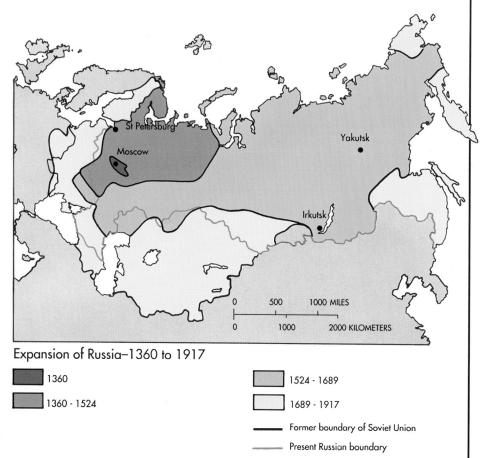

Expansion of Russia–1360 to 1917

- 1360
- 1360 - 1524
- 1524 - 1689
- 1689 - 1917
- —— Former boundary of Soviet Union
- —— Present Russian boundary

Peter and Paul Fortress and Palace Embankment in St. Petersburg (the "window to the west")

New territories

Russia, under Peter the Great, fought Turkey and Sweden, winning Karelia and Estonia on the Baltic Sea. This improved Russia's grip on the Baltic, but in the south Peter was defeated by the Turks. Later, in 1761, Catherine the Great continued the policy of expanding Russia's boundaries. Catherine's armies thrust south and absorbed the lands of the Cossacks, together with the Ukraine and the Crimea on the Black Sea. This gave Russia a warm-water port, important because St. Petersburg and the Baltic ports were closed by ice for five months each year. Russia also made gains when Poland was partitioned in 1772, 1793, and again in 1795. Prussia, Austria, and Russia each took over large tracts of land, while Russia also gained Lithuania and Latvia. Russia built fortified towns in these new territories to maintain central control. In 1773, the Yakutsk Track was opened, linking Irkutsk with Yakutsk.

Achieving power

By the early nineteenth century Russia had become an important European power. This power was further strengthened when Napoleon and his "Grande Armée" invaded Russia in 1812. Despite reaching Moscow, Napoleon was defeated by the freezing Russian winter and by the Russian army led by Tsar Alexander I. By 1900 the Russian Empire was as large as the British, but it was weak in economic and military terms.

Catherine the Great

"Revolution" by Kiriakov depicts the storming of the Winter Palace by the Bolsheviks in 1917.

REVOLUTION

The system of serfdom rigidly bound peasants to the estates of Russian landowners. Serfs had virtually no rights and were often bought and sold with the estates as if they were the property of the landlords. Attempts were made from 1861 onward to get rid of serfdom, but even when it was abolished the former serfs remained as poverty-stricken workers, with little or no political power. The Tsars and the nobility feared that the abolition of

Tsar Alexander II in 1877

serfdom would weaken their authority, so they made sure there was little progress in land reform or measures to improve the situation of the poor. In 1881 Tsar Alexander II

was about to introduce a new constitution to improve conditions when he was assassinated, and so matters went from bad to worse.

From serfdom to starvation

In 1914 Russia became involved in World War I, fighting with Britain, France, and the United States, against Germany and Austria. The war soon exposed the problems of the Russian economy. The railroads were inefficient and unable to maintain a regular supply of troops and equipment to the front. Millions of men were forced to leave the farms to fight with inadequate weapons, clothing, and food. Soon the Tsar's armies were retreating on all fronts. Due to distribution problems, food supplies were restricted. By 1917 starvation was a major problem.

The workers unite

Strikes by workers in March 1917 began in Petrograd but soon spread to Moscow and other big cities. Troops ordered to break the strikes mutinied, and Tsar Nicholas II was forced to abdicate. The provisional government set up by the Duma (parliament) was soon criticized by other political groups. Vladimir Ilyich Lenin, leader of a small political party, called the Bolsheviks, and a prominent revolutionary, returned from Switzerland. The Bolsheviks were very eager to seize power for themselves and they attempted to gain control of the government in July. After their defeat Lenin was forced to go into hiding in Finland. However, the provisional government failed to pursue him and wasted

Workers in Petrograd during the July demonstration of 1917

much time and energy trying to continue the war against Germany.

A revolution

On November 7, 1917, the Bolsheviks struck again, storming the Winter Palace in Moscow and taking control of the country. Lenin established the new communist government, dedicated to improving conditions for the poor, getting rid of the old privileged nobility, and creating a modern and more equal society.

By 1917, starvation and poverty were widespread in Russia.

CIVIL WAR

In 1917 Lenin's Bolshevik Party controlled only part of Russia. The German army occupied some southern regions, and Lenin quickly signed a peace treaty with Germany at Brest-Litovsk. Russia lost a lot of territory as a result of the treaty, but Lenin's priority was to establish his power across the whole expanse of the country.

Red versus white

Alarmed by the communist takeover in Russia, Britain and France had invaded the country in the north and south. At the same time, noncommunist Russian armies were forming with the aim of restoring the Tsar to the throne. These "white" armies, as they were called, soon gained control over parts of western, northern, and southern Russia. To add to the problems of the new "red" government,

Japan had invaded part of Russia's Pacific coast to set up its own independent state. Lenin soon moved the capital back from Petrograd (St. Petersburg) to Moscow, where it was felt to be safer from invasion and attack. The communist government reorganized the Red Army and soon began to push back the invaders. After fierce fighting, the white Russian armies were also finally defeated. This massive civil war between Russians

In 1917, Lenin and his Bolsheviks set out to establish their power across the whole of the country.

caused immense damage to farming. Armies commandeered or simply stole food and animals. Peasants who hid food were killed. People slaughtered their own animals rather than let them be taken over by the armies.

Parade of Russian Army troops in Kharkov, 1920

Communist rule

One of the main aims of the new government was the establishment of communism as soon as possible. This involved the state taking over all land, factories, railroads, ports, and other means of production. Some of the people, especially the peasants, did not like this because they wanted their own land. They had supported the Revolution thinking they would then be able to take over the land previously owned by the nobility. In order to regain the support of the peasants, Lenin in 1921 introduced the New Economic Policy. This recognized people's rights to own some land, and to make a profit. This was vital because in 1921 people in Soviet towns and cities like Moscow were facing starvation. The civil war had destroyed millions of animals, and thousands of acres of land were no longer farmed. This meant that deliveries of food from the country to towns were small and irregular. There were food riots in Moscow. The New Economic Policy quickly increased food production and removed the immediate threat of further civil war.

Soviet Union is born

In December 1922, the communist government established the Union of Soviet Socialist Republics (U.S.S.R.). The union consisted of four union republics – the Russian Republic, Belarussian SSR, Transcaucasia, and the Ukraine. The first republic formed after the Bolshevik revolution, the Russian Republic, was and has always been the largest and most influential in the Soviet Union.

Red Army commanders during the Civil War of 1918-1920

Lenin and his successor, Stalin

STALIN

In 1924, communist leader Vladimir Ilyich Lenin died, and, following a power struggle, Joseph Stalin emerged as the new leader of the Soviet Union. He was determined to turn the country into an important industrial power. To this end he began a policy of developing heavy industries like coal mining, steel making, and engineering. Stalin distrusted the Western countries like Britain and France, because they had tried to invade Russia in 1917. So he decided to develop new industrial areas in the eastern parts of the country.

Stalin's iron grip

In 1928 Stalin ended the New Economic Policy, which had failed to maintain food supplies to the Russian Republic and the rest of the Soviet towns and cities. In its place he introduced a compulsory system of collective farming. Under this system all land, tools, and equipment became the property of the state and were organized into larger, more efficient units called collective farms. The government in Moscow exercised strict control over all collective farms, even deciding what crops should be grown in which fields, and when planting or harvesting should take place. Many peasants resented being forced to join a collective farm, but opposition was brutally crushed by the army and by bands of lawless peasants. Stalin's plan was to modernize and mechanize agriculture. However, Soviet factories concentrated on making tanks, guns, and planes in the 1930s rather than tractors or farm machinery. As a result food was in short supply and millions died in the resulting famine. Stalin maintained an iron grip on the Soviet Union. Any opposition to his plans was ruthlessly suppressed. Constantly warned about a coup by the army, Stalin regularly got rid of senior officers. They were killed, dismissed, or banished to camps in Siberia.

Workers produce more tanks for the front during World War II.

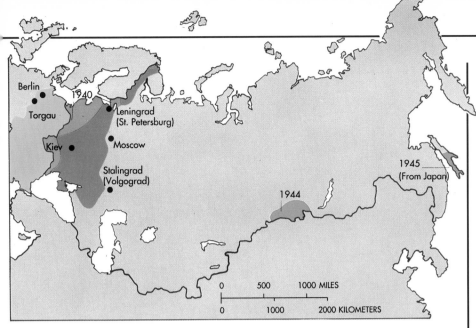

The U.S.S.R. in World War II

▨ Territory gained by the U.S.S.R

▨ Farthest advance of German forces

▨ Farthest advance of Soviet forces

— Former boundary of Soviet Union

World War II
In 1939, Stalin signed a nonaggression pact with the newly powerful Nazi Germany. The aim was to give the Soviet Union more time to build up its armed forces in preparation for what Stalin saw as a future German invasion. In 1941, Germany launched a massive invasion of the Soviet Union led by Adolf Hitler. Despite the time gained by the nonaggression pact the Red Army was still not prepared for the German onslaught. The Soviet troops were forced to fall back toward Moscow. As they retreated, the Red Army carried out a scorched-earth policy, which involved burning all crops, killing all animals, and disabling all machinery. The Russian winter came to the aid of the country and the German advance was finally halted at Stalingrad, now called Volgograd, in 1943. The Red Army began to advance westward, and pursued the retreating Nazi army into Hungary, Poland, Czechoslovakia, and even Germany itself, finally capturing Berlin. Over 30 million Soviet people died during World War II, and millions more were wounded.

A Europe divided
Shortly before the end of the war in 1945, the leaders of Britain, the United States, and the Soviet Union met to divide up Europe among themselves. Stalin wanted to push communist influence as far west as possible, making the Soviet Union a power to rival the United States.

Russia joins with Britain and the United States to defeat Hitler.

The Soviet Union celebrates 60 years of communist rule with a parade in Red Square, Moscow.

COLD WAR

Although the Soviet Union and the United States had fought together to defeat the Germans, from 1945 onward the two superpowers became rivals. The Americans and other Western people were worried by the spread of communism across Europe, and by the new Soviet nuclear weapons program. After 1945, Europe was divided by what Winston Churchill called an "iron curtain." To the west were Britain, France, West Germany, and the United States. To the east was the group led by the Soviet Union, a military alliance called the Warsaw Pact, made up of Poland, East Germany, Hungary, Bulgaria, Czechoslovakia, and Romania. This period of rivalry between the Soviet Union and the West was called the "Cold War."

In 1961, Yuri Gagarin became the first man to orbit the earth.

The temperature drops

The Soviet Union and the United States began the space race after the Soviet Union put Yuri Gagarin into space in 1961. There was also great competition

Mikhail Gorbachev listens to the people's reactions to *perestroika*.

between the two countries in building up their powerful nuclear missiles. Each country wanted the newest and best weapons. The Soviet Union continued to support uprisings against Western-style governments, and crushed any uprisings against the Soviet system. In 1956 there were riots in Hungary against the communist government. The Soviet

army led the Warsaw Pact troops that halted the riots. The same happened in Czechoslovakia in 1968. The problems within the Soviet Union also continued. Stalin died in

1953 and was eventually replaced by Nikita Khrushchev. Despite massive efforts there was never enough quality milk, meat, fruit, or bread in the stores. In 1964 Khrushchev was replaced in a coup by Leonid Brezhnev and Aleksei Kosygin who continued the Cold War policy with the United States. With a brief interval during the 1970s, the Cold War continued until 1985.

Perestroika

In 1985 Mikhail Gorbachev became the new leader of the Soviet Union. He inherited a country in crisis. The economy had been weakened by overspending on weapons, and agriculture was in a poor state, with food having to be rationed as a result. Gorbachev's policy of *perestroika*, which means restructuring, brought an end to the Cold War and encouraged negotiations with the United States. A reduction in arms meant that more money was available for the growth of agriculture and industry. Gorbachev reduced the massive state spending on tanks, planes, ships, and nuclear weapons and gave the people more control over the farms and factories. Previously, ministries in Moscow controlled all aspects of people's lives. Now many of them were able to become cooperatives or privately owned. At the same time, Gorbachev's policy of *glasnost*, or openness as it is called, gave people greater freedom to express their views. Political prisoners like Andrei Sakharov were finally freed.

TOWARD INDEPENDENCE

Arms control treaties were signed with the United States in 1987, 1989, and 1991, all reducing both conventional and nuclear weapons. Countries like Poland, Hungary, East Germany, and Czechoslovakia experienced growing pressure for greater democracy. People held marches and parades, and there were even riots. Gorbachev allowed these movements to grow, and one by one, between 1989 and 1990, free elections were held creating new, democratic, noncommunist governments in most East European countries. The opening of the Berlin Wall in 1989 was hailed as an historic event symbolizing the collapse of communism in Eastern Europe. Within the Soviet Union, demands for democracy were also influencing changes. Powerful movements in the Soviet Union had long demanded greater freedom from central government. Such movements began to gain strength during the late 1980s, particularly in the Baltic republics of Estonia, Latvia, and Lithuania. In 1990, Lithuania declared independence, and Estonia and Latvia called for gradual separation from the Soviet Union. By the end of 1990, all fifteen republics had declared that their own laws took precedence over those of the central government.

The fifteen republics held their first free elections in 1991, in which many noncommunists were elected. Boris Yeltsin became president of Russia, the largest and most influential republic.

Black, white, and red all over
Pravda (Truth) was for three quarters of a century the daily newspaper of the all-powerful Communist Party. At its height it was compulsory reading for all party members and its circulation was 13 million.

Founded by Lenin in 1912, the paper prospered under the system of huge state subsidies for newsprint, ink, machinery, and distribution costs, and became the owner of a vast publishing empire.

The future of *Pravda* was shaky during Gorbachev's *perestroika,* when subscription ceased to be compulsory and circulation fell drastically. Boris Yeltsin even banned the paper for a week, but *Pravda* bounced back, reemerging as an independent daily without Lenin on its front page or its former slogan "Proletariat of the World Unite."

Today Pravda is foreign owned, after closing briefly in 1992 , and still appears regularly.

Boris Yeltsin addresses crowds of supporters after the failed coup of August 1991.

A military coup

On August 20, 1991, hardline, old-style communists tried to stage a military coup in the Soviet Union. They arrested President Gorbachev at his vacation home in the Crimea, and declared an end to *perestroika* and *glasnost*. They feared that the Soviet Union was disintegrating and that the central power of the Communist Party was being destroyed. Boris Yeltsin and the newly elected Russian parliament led the opposition to the coup. When military leaders refused to order their troops to fire on civilians the coup failed, and its leaders were themselves arrested. A shaken President Gorbachev returned to Moscow on August 23.

Communism fades

The coup accelerated events that were already underway. The leaders of the republics were eager to destroy the power of the Communist Party, which was banned in large parts of Russia in September 1991. The fifteen republics agreed to formally end the communist Soviet Union in December 1991.

The communist state, established by Lenin in 1917, was thus formally destroyed. Eleven of the republics agreed to form a Commonwealth of Independent States (C.I.S.) led by Russia, which would have fairly limited powers over the rest of the independent republics. Lithuania, Latvia, Estonia, and Georgia chose not to join, retaining complete independence.

OUTLOOK

The economic crisis in Moscow reveals itself through the empty shelves and spiraling food prices.

Boris Yeltsin's power increased as that of Mikhail Gorbachev decreased. From December 1991, Gorbachev had no country to lead, and as president of the Russian Federation, Boris Yeltsin is now confronting the immense problems that face his country's transition to a market economy. Yeltsin argued the need to continue arms reduction and to modernize agriculture and industry. However, he knows that Russian people want to see some positive benefits from all the changes, especially more goods in the stores.

Inflation is currently surging toward 1,000 percent per year, and previous food shortages have now been replaced by soaring prices. Wages, however, are not rising at the same rate, threatening a large-scale descent into starvation. The situation in Russia and the other former Soviet republics is not unlike that in postwar Europe. The economies of the states are spinning dangerously out of control, and aid has been promised from the Western world. Financial packages, which aim to help stabilize the economy, have been promised from the International Monetary Fund (I.M.F.) and the World Bank.

Cracking up

Russia has set out to establish itself as the logical successor to the Soviet Union. However, serious problems remain. There are continuing disputes between the states over control of Soviet nuclear weapons, the Red Army, and the Soviet Navy. Many Russians do not like the sweeping powers Yeltsin has been given to carry out his reforms.

A breakup of Russia itself was prevented by Boris Yeltsin when all but two of its constituents signed a Federation Treaty in 1992. Chechenya-Ingush and

Decontamination of vehicle at Chernobyl

Tatarstan, however, have yet to sign, highlighting the dangers facing the entire territory of the former Soviet Union.

What price nuclear?

Nuclear accidents and waste have made parts of the Russian territory uninhabitable for decades to come. Cleanup programs will cost huge sums, and many Russians have been uprooted for resettlement in safe areas. Decades of nuclear mishaps, such as the 1986 Chernobyl disaster, and dumping of waste, were covered up by the former Soviet communist government.

Boris Yeltsin

Boris Nikolayevich Yeltsin is president of the Russian Federation. He became head of the republic in 1990 when he was elected chairman by the republic's Congress of People's Deputies. In 1991, he was elected to the newly created post of president by the voters. Yeltsin had called for radical social, economic, and political changes in the former Soviet Union and criticized the Soviet leader Mikhail Gorbachev for moving too slowly change the economy.

Yeltsin was born in Sverdlovsk in 1931, and joined the Communist Party in 1961. In 1976 he became head of the Party organization in Sverdlovsk, and in 1985 Gorbachev appointed him chief of the Communist Party organization in Moscow, where he became a member of the ruling party's Politburo. He was removed from these posts in 1987 for his criticism of Gorbachev. In 1989 he won a seat in the new Soviet government, but his bid for the leadership was opposed by Gorbachev. Yeltsin resigned from the Communist Party in 1990.

In August 1991 he led popular opposition to a coup against Gorbachev, and became powerful and famous at home and abroad.

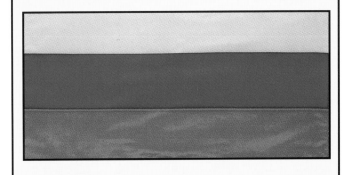

FACTS AND FIGURES

Name: The Russian Federation.

Area: 6,591,104 sq.miles (17,070,959 sq km).

Capital: Moscow.

Currency: The ruble. One hundred kopecks make one ruble.

Population: 146,386,000.

Population density: 21 people per square mile (8.1 per sq km).

Birthrate: 14.7 per 1,000.

Deathrate: 11.2 per 1,000.

Size: Maximum east-west extent is 5,770 miles (9,286 km). Maximum north-south extent is 3,000 miles (4,828 km).

Deepest lake: Lake Baikal, 5,750 feet (1,753 meters) deep, 400 miles (643 km) long, and 50 miles (80 km) wide.

Highest mountain: Mount Elbrus, 18,579 feet (5,663 m).

Longest rivers: Lena, 2,730 miles (4,393 km). Irtysh, 2,632 miles (4,236 km). Ob, 2,265 miles (3,646 km). Volga, 2,190 miles (3,524 km).

Physical features: Much of the country is low plain. Highest mountains are

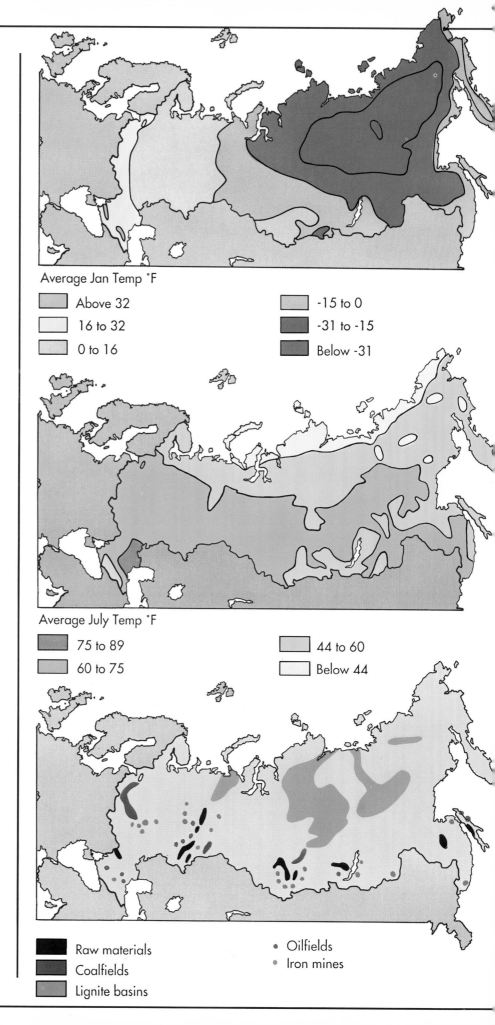

Average Jan Temp °F

- Above 32
- 16 to 32
- 0 to 16
- -15 to 0
- -31 to -15
- Below -31

Average July Temp °F

- 75 to 89
- 60 to 75
- 44 to 60
- Below 44

- Raw materials
- Coalfields
- Lignite basins
- Oilfields
- Iron mines

the Caucasus and scattered parts of eastern Siberia. Low Ural Mountains in central part of the country form traditional boundary between Europe and Asia.

Largest city: Moscow. Population of 8,769,000.

Ethnic breakdown: Russian 83 %, Ukranian 7%, Kazakh, 4%, Others 6%.

Language: Russian. Many local languages are also spoken throughout the country. Most of the Russian population speak a Slavic language – Russian, Ukranian, or Belarussian – as their first language.

Religion: Russian Orthodox though others such as Roman Catholicism, Islam, and Judaism are practiced.

Largest cities: Moscow – population 8,769,000. St. Petersburg – population 4,295,000. Nizhnii-Novgorod (formerly Gorki) – population 1,392,000. Novosibirsk – population 1,384,000.

Other Russian towns and cities:

Novgorod – Ancient city founded in mid-800s. Contains splendid Russian architecture and paintings from 1000s to 1700s.

Yaroslavl – Large port on the Volga. Manufactures engines and tires. Historic churches with beautiful murals and frescoes.

Vladimir – Outstanding architectural monuments, including two-story Golden Gate and Dimitri Cathedral, with its intricately carved high reliefs.

Orel – City containing many fine literary museums. Once home to Ivan Bunin, Leonid Andreyev, and other notable Russian writers.

Kazan – Center of industry and culture, with its history and fine arts museums, and Kazan University.

Ulyanovsk – Lenin's birthplace. Contains many museums celebrating his life.

Volgograd – Formerly Stalingrad, it is a major port and industrial center. A huge monument at Mamai Mound honors the Soviet victory over German troops at the battle of Stalingrad.

Climate statistics:

	January temp.	July temp.	Annual rainfall
Archangel	-2 deg. F	46 deg. F	16.8 inches
Moscow	18 deg. F	66 deg. F	20.9 inches
Yakutsk	-49 deg. F	60 deg. F	13.7 inches

Russia's percentage share of gas, oil, grain, and steel output within the former Soviet Union in 1990.

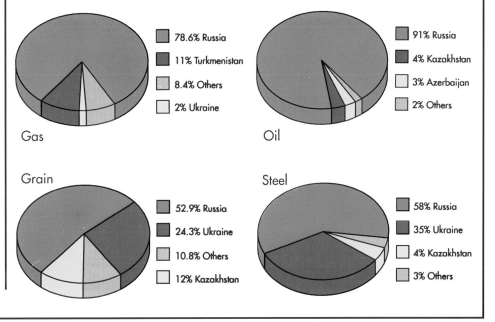

Gas
- 78.6% Russia
- 11% Turkmenistan
- 8.4% Others
- 2% Ukraine

Oil
- 91% Russia
- 4% Kazakhstan
- 3% Azerbaijan
- 2% Others

Grain
- 52.9% Russia
- 24.3% Ukraine
- 10.8% Others
- 12% Kazakhstan

Steel
- 58% Russia
- 35% Ukraine
- 4% Kazakhstan
- 3% Others

CHRONOLOGY AND FAMOUS PEOPLE

862 Novgorod becomes capital of Rus
1242 Battle on the ice ensures survival of Novgorod against invaders
1326 The center of the Orthodox Church is moved from Kiev to Moscow
1480 Ivan III (the Great) finally defeats Tatars, and absorbs Tver and Vyatka into Muscovy

Catherine the Great (1729 -1796) Empress of Russia, she was devoted to the arts, promoting culture in Russia.

1552 Russians capture Kazan from Tatars and start the trek east to the Pacific
1648 Traders reach the Pacific Ocean
1682-1725 Peter the Great modernizes Russia with Western European technology and ideas
1761-96 Catherine the Great expands Russia south to the Black Sea
1861 Alexander II frees serfs, but most continue to live in great poverty. Alexander murdered by revolutionaries in 1881
1894 Nicholas II becomes Tsar
1905 Japan defeats Russia in the Pacific war and after internal riots and unrest Nicholas reestablishes his power
1914 World War I starts. Russian armies defeated and millions killed and injured
1917 The Tsar is forced to abdicate and the provisional government takes over. In November the Bolshevik Party led by Lenin seizes power
1918 Civil war begins between the Red Army and White armies, some of whom support the Tsar. Russia makes peace with Germany
1920 Red Army finally wins the civil war after two years of fighting

Vladimir Ilyich Lenin (1870 -1924) He founded the Communist Party and set up the world's first Communist dictatorship. He ruled from 1917 until his death.

Joseph Stalin (1879 - 1953) Dictator from 1929 until 1953, he ruled by terror. Stalin changed the Soviet Union into one of the world's industrial and military powers.

Leonid Brezhnev (1906 - 1982) Headed the Soviet Union from 1964 until his death, increasing military strength and ordering the invasion of Afghanistan in 1979.

Mikhail Gorbachev (1931 -) President from 1985 to 1990. He won the Nobel Peace Prize for his contribution to world peace, becoming internationally famous.

1921 New Economic Policy aims to aid economic recovery
1924 Lenin dies and is succeeded by Stalin
1928 Stalin begins enforced collectivization. Millions of peasants resist and are killed
1941 German invasion of Soviet Union
1943 German army defeated at Stalingrad
1945 Germany defeated. Soviet troops occupy East Germany, Poland, Hungary, and Czechoslovakia. All become Soviet states with Romania and Yugoslavia
1946 The Cold War begins as the Soviet Union and the United States disagree about the future development of Europe
1953 Krushchev takes over as Soviet leader after Stalin dies
1962 The Soviet Union is forced to withdraw missiles from Cuba
1964 Krushchev is ousted and replaced by Brezhnev and Kosygin
1972 Brezhnev and U.S. President Nixon sign an arms control agreement
1979 Soviet Union sends troops into Afghanistan
1982 Brezhnev dies and is replaced by Andropov
1984 Andropov dies and is replaced by the elderly Konstantin Chernenko

Boris Yeltsin (1931 -) Famous for his inspired leadership during a coup attempt against Gorbachev. Yeltsin became leader of a newly independent Russia.

1985 Chernenko dies and Gorbachev replaces him
1986 Gorbachev begins policies of *perestroika* and *glasnost*
1987 Arms reduction treaty signed between Soviet Union and U.S.A.
1988 Soviet Army withdraws from Afghanistan
1989 Yeltsin elected leader of Russia
1991 Coup to overthrow Gorbachev fails. Yeltsin gains influence
1991 Eleven republics form the C.I.S.
1992 A Federation Treaty is signed by 15 Russian republics

INDEX

PHOTOCREDITS

All the pictures in this book were supplied by Novosti R.I.A.
apart from the front cover and pages 6 both, 13, 22 top, 24,
25, 26, 27 both, 31 top left & bottom: Frank Spooner Pictures;
pages 10 bottom & 12: The Hulton Picture Company; page 20
bottom: Mary Evans Picture Library.